Native American Wisdom

Native American Wisdom

Compiled by
KENT NERBURN, PH.D.
and
LOUISE MENGELKOCH, M.A.

THE CLASSIC WISDOM COLLECTION
NEW WORLD LIBRARY
NOVATO, CALIFORNIA

The Classic Wisdom Collection
New World Library
14 Pamaron Way, Novato, CA 94949

Cover design: Greg Wittrock
Text design: Nancy Benedict
Typography: Wilsted & Taylor

Library of Congress Cataloging-in-Publication Data
Native American wisdom / compiled by
Kent Nerburn and Louise Mengelkoch.
p. cm. — (The classic wisdom collection)
ISBN 0-93142-78-2 (acid-free paper)
1. Indians of North America—Philosophy.
2. Indians of North America—Religion
and mythology.
I. Nerburn, Kent, 1946-
II. Mengelkoch, Louise. III. Series

E98.P5N38 1991   91-21315
191'.08997—dc20   CIP

First printing, October 1991
ISBN 978-0-931432-78-1
Printed in Canada
30 29 28 27 26 25 24 23

"There is a dignity about the social intercourse of old Indians which reminds me of a stroll through a winter forest."

Frederick Remington

Contents

CONTENTS

Publisher's Preface

Life is an endless cycle of change. We and our world will never remain the same.

Every generation has difficulty relating to the previous generation; even the language changes. The child speaks a different language than the parent does.

It seems almost miraculous, then, that certain voices, certain books, are able to speak not only to one, but to many generations beyond them. The plays and poems of William Shakespeare are still relevant today—still capable of giving us goose bumps, still entertaining, disturbing, and profound. Shakespeare is the writer who, in the English language, defines the word *classic*.

There are many other writers and thinkers who, for a great many reasons, can be considered classic, for they withstand the test of time. We want to present the best of them to you in the New World Library Classic Wisdom Collection. Even though these writers and thinkers lived many years ago, they are still relevant and important in today's world for the enduring words of wisdom they created, words that should forever be kept in print.

Native American Wisdom is a very special book in this collection. It is profound, enlightened, touching, poetic, and inspired. Every citizen of the planet Earth can gain value from the words and insights of the native Americans.

We pray that their traditions will be remembered, and will grow and prosper; we hope that this book will, in its own way, contribute to increased awareness of and respect for the wisdom of the native American people.

A significant percentage of the profits of this book will be contributed to worthwhile organizations dedicated to improving the quality of life of native Americans and preserving their traditions and wisdom.

Shakti Gawain
Marc Allen
New World Library

Introduction

In 1492 Columbus and his crew, lost, battered, and stricken with dysentery, were helped ashore by a people he described as "neither black nor white . . . fairly tall, good looking and well proportioned." Believing he had landed in the East Indies, he called these people Indians. In fact, they were part of a great population that had made its home on this continent for centuries.

The inhabitants of this land were not one people. Their customs differed. Their languages differed. Some tilled the earth; others hunted and picked the abundance of the land around them. They lived in different kinds of housing and governed themselves according to differing rules.

But they shared in common a belief that the earth is a spiritual presence that must be honored, not mastered. Unfortunately, western Europeans who came to these shores had a contrary belief. To them, the entire American continent was a beautiful but savage land that it was not only their right, but their duty, to tame and use as they saw fit.

As the twentieth century draws to a close, Western civilization is confronting the inevitable results of this European-American philosophy of dominance. We have gotten out of balance with our earth, and the very future of our planet depends on our capacity to restore that balance.

We are crying out for help, for a grounding in the truth of nature, for words of wisdom. That wisdom is here, contained in the words of the native peoples of the Americas. But these people speak quietly. Their words are simple and their voices soft. We have not heard them because we have not taken the time to listen. Perhaps now the time is right for us to open our ears and hearts to the words they have to say.

Unlike many traditions, the spiritual wisdom of the native American is not found in a set of "scriptural" materials. It is, and always has been, a part of the fabric of daily life and experience. One of the most poignant reflections of this spiritual message is found in their tradition of oratory.

Traditionally, Indians did not carry on dialogues when discussing important matters. Rather, each person listened attentively until his or her turn came to speak, and then he or she rose and spoke without interruption about the heart of the matter under consideration. This tradition produced a measured eloquence of speech and thought that is almost unmatched for its clarity and simplicity.

Indian reasoning about governmental and social affairs was also carried on with the same uncompromising purity of insight and expression.

It is from these orations, recorded observations of life and social affairs, and other first-person testimonies that the materials for this book have been drawn. This wisdom has been available in written form for some time, but much of it has been recorded only in imposing governmental documents and arcane academic treatises.

We hope this volume breathes life back into these timeless words. As meditations, they have much to teach, not only about our personal lives and relationships, but about affairs of state and international relations as well. The time has come to listen to these echoes from our land—the wisdom and teaching of the native American people.

Kent Nerburn
Louise Mengelkoch

Native American Wisdom

1

The Ways of the Land

*"All things are connected. Whatever befalls the
earth befalls the children of the earth."*

Chief Seattle
Suqwamish and Duwamish

I was born in Nature's wide domain! The trees
were all that sheltered my infant limbs, the blue
heavens all that covered me. I am one of Nature's
children. I have always admired her. She shall be
my glory: her features, her robes, and the wreath
about her brow, the seasons, her stately oaks, and
the evergreen—her hair, ringlets over the earth—
all contribute to my enduring love of her.

And wherever I see her, emotions of pleasure
roll in my breast, and swell and burst like waves on
the shores of the ocean, in prayer and praise to
Him who has placed me in her hand. It is thought
great to be born in palaces, surrounded with

1

wealth—but to be born in Nature's wide domain is greater still!

I would much more glory in this birthplace, with the broad canopy of heaven above me, and the giant arms of the forest trees for my shelter, than to be born in palaces of marble, studded with pillars of gold! Nature will be Nature still, while palaces shall decay and fall in ruins.

Yes, Niagara will be Niagara a thousand years hence! The rainbow, a wreath over her brow, shall continue as long as the sun, and the flowing of the river—while the work of art, however carefully protected and preserved, shall fade and crumble into dust!

George Copway (Kahgegagahbowh)
Ojibwe

What is man without the beasts? If all the beasts were gone, men would die from great loneliness of spirit, for whatever happens to the beasts also happens to man. All things are connected. Whatever befalls the earth befalls the children of the earth.

Chief Seattle
Suqwamish and Duwamish

I love that land of winding waters more than all the rest of the world. A man who would not love his father's grave is worse than a wild animal.

Chief Joseph
Nez Perce

The character of the Indian's emotion left little room in his heart for antagonism toward his fellow creatures. . . . For the Lakota [one of the three branches of the Sioux nation], mountains, lakes, rivers, springs, valleys, and woods were all finished beauty. Winds, rain, snow, sunshine, day, night, and change of seasons were endlessly fascinating. Birds, insects, and animals filled the world with knowledge that defied the comprehension of man.

The Lakota was a true naturalist—a lover of Nature. He loved the earth and all things of the earth, and the attachment grew with age. The old people came literally to love the soil and they sat or reclined on the ground with a feeling of being close to a mothering power.

It was good for the skin to touch the earth, and the old people liked to remove their moccasins and walk with bare feet on the sacred earth.

Their tipis were built upon the earth and their

3

altars were made of earth. The birds that flew in the air came to rest upon the earth, and it was the final abiding place of all things that lived and grew. The soil was soothing, strengthening, cleansing, and healing.

This is why the old Indian still sits upon the earth instead of propping himself up and away from its life-giving forces. For him, to sit or lie upon the ground is to be able to think more deeply and to feel more keenly; he can see more clearly into the mysteries of life and come closer in kinship to other lives about him.

Chief Luther Standing Bear
Teton Sioux

You ask me to plow the ground. Shall I take a knife and tear my mother's bosom? Then when I die she will not take me to her bosom to rest.

You ask me to dig for stones! Shall I dig under her skin for her bones? Then when I die I cannot enter her body to be born again.

You ask me to cut grass and make hay and sell it, and be rich like white men, but how dare I cut my mother's hair?

I want my people to stay with me here. All the

dead men will come to life again. Their spirits will come to their bodies again. We must wait here in the homes of our fathers and be ready to meet them in the bosom of our mother.

Wovoka
Paiute

Great Spirit—I want no blood upon my land to stain the grass. I want it all clear and pure, and I wish it so, that all who go through among my people may find it peaceful when they come, and leave peacefully when they go.

Ten Bears
Yamparika Comanche

I love the land and the buffalo and will not part with it. . . .

I want the children raised as I was . . . I don't want to settle. I love to roam over the prairies. There I feel free and happy, but when we settle down we grow pale and die.

Satanta
Kiowa Chief

2

The Ways of Words and Silence

"It does not require many words to speak the truth."

> *Chief Joseph*
> *Nez Perce*

The first American mingled with his pride a singular humility. Spiritual arrogance was foreign to his nature and teaching. He never claimed that his power of articulate speech was proof of superiority over "dumb creation"; on the other hand, speech is to him a perilous gift.

He believes profoundly in silence—the sign of a perfect equilibrium. Silence is the absolute poise or balance of body, mind, and spirit.

The man who preserves his selfhood ever calm and unshaken by the storms of existence—not a leaf, as it were, astir on the tree, not a ripple upon the surface of the shining pool—his, in the mind of the unlettered sage, is the ideal attitude and conduct of life. . . .

Silence is the cornerstone of character.

Charles Alexander Eastman (Ohiyesa)
Santee Sioux

Silence was meaningful with the Lakota, and his granting a space of silence before talking was done in the practice of true politeness and regardful of the rule that "thought comes before speech."

And in the midst of sorrow, sickness, death, or misfortune of any kind, and in the presence of the notable and great, silence was the mark of respect. More powerful than words was silence with the Lakota.

His strict observance of this tenet of good behavior was the reason, no doubt, for his being given the false characterization by the white man of being a stoic. He has been judged to be dumb, stupid, indifferent, and unfeeling.

As a matter of truth, he was the most sympathetic of men, but his emotions of depth and sincerity were tempered with control. Silence meant to the Lakota what it meant to Disraeli when he said, "Silence is the mother of truth," for the silent man was ever to be trusted, while the man ever ready with speech was never taken seriously.

Chief Luther Standing Bear
Teton Sioux

In my opinion, it was chiefly owing to their deep contemplation in their silent retreats in the days of youth that the old Indian orators acquired the habit of carefully arranging their thoughts.

They listened to the warbling of birds and noted the grandeur and the beauties of the forest. The majestic clouds—which appear like mountains of granite floating in the air—the golden tints of a summer evening sky, and all the changes of nature, possessed a mysterious significance.

All this combined to furnish ample matter for reflection to the contemplating youth.

Francis Assikinack (Blackbird)
Ottawa

Because we are old, it may be thought that the memory of things may be lost with us, who have not, like you, the art of preserving it by committing all transactions to writing.

We nevertheless have methods of transmitting from father to son an account of all these things. You will find the remembrance of them is faithfully preserved, and our succeeding generations are made acquainted with what has passed, that it may not be forgot as long as the earth remains.

Kanickhungo
Treaty negotiations with Six Nations

You must speak straight so that your words may go as sunlight into our hearts.

Cochise ("Like Ironweed")
Chiricahua Chief

A treaty, in the minds of our people, is an eternal word. Events often make it seem expedient to depart from the pledged word, but we are conscious that the first departure creates a logic for the second departure, until there is nothing left of the word.

Declaration of Indian Purpose (1961)
American Indian Chicago Conference

I believe much trouble and blood would be saved if we opened our hearts more. I will tell you in my way how the Indian sees things. The white man has more words to tell you how they look to him, but it does not require many words to speak the truth.

Chief Joseph
Nez Perce

Good words do not last long unless they amount to something. Words do not pay for my dead people. They do not pay for my country, now overrun by white men. They do not protect my father's grave. They do not pay for all my horses and cattle.

Good words will not give me back my children. Good words will not make good the promise of your War Chief. Good words will not give my people good health and stop them from dying. Good words will not get my people a home where they can live in peace and take care of themselves.

I am tired of talk that comes to nothing. It makes my heart sick when I remember all the good words and all the broken promises. There has been too much talking by men who had no right to talk.

Chief Joseph
Nez Perce

How smooth must be the language of the whites, when they can make right look like wrong, and wrong like right.

Black Hawk
Sauk

My father, you have made promises to me and to my children. If the promises had been made by a person of no standing, I should not be surprised to see his promises fail. But you, who are so great in riches and in power, I am astonished that I do not see your promises fulfilled!

I would have been better pleased if you had never made such promises, than that you should have made them and not performed them. . . .

Shinguaconse ("Little Pine")

3

The Ways of Learning

"Knowledge was inherent in all things. The world was a library. . . ."

> *Chief Luther Standing Bear*
> *Oglala Sioux*

Look at me—I am poor and naked, but I am the chief of the nation. We do not want riches, but we do want to train our children right. Riches would do us no good. We could not take them with us to the other world. We do not want riches. We want peace and love.

> *Red Cloud*
> Sioux

You who are so wise must know that different nations have different conceptions of things. You will not therefore take it amiss if our ideas of the white man's kind of education happens not to be the same as yours. We have had some experience of it.

Several of our young people were brought up in your colleges. They were instructed in all your sciences; but, when they came back to us, they were bad runners, ignorant of every means of living in the woods, unable to bear either cold or hunger. They didn't know how to build a cabin, take a deer, or kill an enemy. They spoke our language imperfectly.

They were therefore unfit to be hunters, warriors, or counsellors; they were good for nothing.

We are, however, not the less obliged for your kind offer, though we decline accepting it. To show our gratefulness, if the gentlemen of Virginia shall send us a dozen of their sons, we will take great care with their education, instruct them in all we know, and make men of them.

Canassatego
Treaty of Lancaster

It was our belief that the love of possessions is a weakness to be overcome. Its appeal is to the material part, and if allowed its way, it will in time disturb one's spiritual balance. Therefore, children must early learn the beauty of generosity. They are taught to give what they prize most, that they may taste the happiness of giving.

If a child is inclined to be grasping, or to cling to any of his or her little possessions, legends are related about the contempt and disgrace falling upon the ungenerous and mean person. . . .

The Indians in their simplicity literally give away all that they have—to relatives, to guests of other tribes or clans, but above all to the poor and the aged, from whom they can hope for no return.

Charles Alexander Eastman (Ohiyesa)
Santee Sioux

The Indians were religious from the first moments of life. From the moment of the mother's recognition that she had conceived to the end of the child's second year of life, which was the ordinary duration of lactation, it was supposed by us that the mother's spiritual influence was supremely important.

Her attitude and secret meditations must be such as to instill into the receptive soul of the unborn child the love of the Great Mystery and a sense of connectedness with all creation. Silence and isolation are the rule of life for the expectant mother.

She wanders prayerful in the stillness of great

woods, or on the bosom of the untrodden prairie, and to her poetic mind the imminent birth of her child prefigures the advent of a hero—a thought conceived in the virgin breast of primeval nature, and dreamed out in a hush that is broken only by the sighing of the pine tree or the thrilling orchestra of a distant waterfall.

And when the day of days in her life dawns—the day in which there is to be a new life, the miracle of whose making has been entrusted to her—she seeks no human aid. She has been trained and prepared in body and mind for this, her holiest duty, ever since she can remember.

Childbirth is best met alone, where no curious embarrass her, where all nature says to her spirit: "It's love! It's love! The fulfilling of life!" When a sacred voice comes to her out of the silence, and a pair of eyes open upon her in the wilderness, she knows with joy that she has borne well her part in the great song of creation!

Presently she returns to the camp, carrying the mysterious, the holy, the dearest bundle! She feels the endearing warmth of it and hears its soft breathing. It is still a part of herself, since both are nourished by the same mouthful, and no look of a lover could be sweeter than its deep, trusting gaze.

She continues her spiritual teaching, at first silently—a mere pointing of the index finger to nature—then in whispered songs, bird-like, at morning and evening. To her and to the child the birds are real people, who live very close to the Great Mystery; the murmuring trees breathe its presence; the falling waters chant its praise.

If the child should chance to be fretful, the mother raises her hand. "Hush! Hush!" she cautions it tenderly, "The spirits may be disturbed!" She bids it be still and listen—listen to the silver voice of the aspen, or the clashing cymbals of the birch; and at night she points to the heavenly blazed trail through nature's galaxy of splendor to nature's God. Silence, love, reverence—this is the trinity of first lessons, and to these she later adds generosity, courage, and chastity.

Charles Alexander Eastman (Ohiyesa)
Santee Sioux

Children were taught that true politeness was to be defined in actions rather than in words. They were never allowed to pass between the fire and an older person or a visitor, to speak while others were speaking, or to make fun of a crippled or disfigured person. If a child thoughtlessly tried to do so, a parent, in a quiet voice, immediately set him right.

Expressions such as "excuse me," "pardon me," and "so sorry," now so often lightly and unnecessarily used, are not in the Lakota language. If one chanced to injure or cause inconvenience to another, the word *wanunhecun*, or "mistake," was spoken. This was sufficient to indicate that no discourtesy was intended and that what had happened was accidental.

Our young people, raised under the old rules of courtesy, never indulged in the present habit of talking incessantly and all at the same time. To do so would have been not only impolite, but foolish; for poise, so much admired as a social grace, could not be accompanied by restlessness. Pauses were acknowledged gracefully and did not cause lack of ease or embarrassment.

In talking to children, the old Lakota would place a hand on the ground and explain: "We sit in the lap of our Mother. From her we, and all other living things, come. We shall soon pass, but the place where we now rest will last forever." So we, too, learned to sit or lie on the ground and become conscious of life about us in its multitude of forms.

Sometimes we boys would sit motionless and watch the swallows, the tiny ants, or perhaps some small animal at its work and ponder its industry and ingenuity; or we lay on our backs and looked long at the sky, and when the stars came out made shapes from the various groups.

Everything was possessed of personality, only differing from us in form. Knowledge was inherent in all things. The world was a library and its books were the stones, leaves, grass, brooks, and the birds and animals that shared, alike with us, the storms and blessings of earth. We learned to do what only the student of nature ever learns, and that was to feel beauty. We never railed at the storms, the furious winds, and the biting frosts and snows. To do so intensified human futility, so whatever came we adjusted ourselves, by more effort and energy if necessary, but without complaint.

Even the lightning did us no harm, for whenever it came too close, mothers and grandmothers in every tipi put cedar leaves on the coals and their magic kept danger away. Bright days and dark days were both expressions of the Great Mystery, and the Indian reveled in being close to the Great Holiness.

Observation was certain to have its rewards. Interest, wonder, admiration grew, and the fact was appreciated that life was more than mere human manifestation; it was expressed in a multitude of forms.

This appreciation enriched Lakota existence. Life was vivid and pulsing; nothing was casual and commonplace. The Indian lived—lived in every sense of the word—from his first to his last breath.

Chief Luther Standing Bear
Teton Sioux

What boy would not be an Indian for a while when he thinks of the freest life in the world? We were close students of nature. We studied the habits of animals just as you study your books. We watched the men of our people and acted like them in our play, then learned to emulate them in our lives.

No people have better use of their five senses than the children of the wilderness. We could smell as well as hear and see. We could feel and taste as well as we could see and hear. Nowhere has the memory been more fully developed than in the wild life.

As a little child, it was instilled into me to be silent and reticent. This was one of the most important traits to form in the character of the Indian. As a hunter and warrior, it was considered absolutely necessary to him, and was thought to lay the foundations of patience and self-control. There are times when boisterous mirth is indulged in by our people, but the rule is gravity and decorum.

I wished to be a brave man as much as a white boy desires to be a great lawyer or even president of the United States.

I was made to respect the adults, especially the aged. I was not allowed to join in their discussions, or even to speak in their presence, unless requested to do so. Indian etiquette was very strict, and among the requirements was that of avoiding direct address. A term of relationship or some title of courtesy was commonly used instead of the personal name by those who wished to show respect.

We were taught generosity to the poor and reverence for the Great Mystery. Religion was the basis of all Indian training.

Charles Alexander Eastman (Ohiyesa)
Santee Sioux

We send our little Indian boys and girls to school, and when they come back talking English, they come back swearing. There is no swear word in the Indian languages, and I haven't yet learned to swear.

Gertrude S. Bonnin (Zitkala-Sa)
Yankton Sioux

4

The Ways of Living

"Our fathers gave us many laws, which they had learned from their fathers. These laws were good."

Chief Joseph
Nez Perce

Our fathers gave us many laws, which they had learned from their fathers. These laws were good. They told us to treat all people as they treated us; that we should never be the first to break a bargain; that it was a disgrace to tell a lie; that we should speak only the truth; that it was a shame for one man to take from another his wife or his property without paying for it.

We were taught to believe that the Great Spirit sees and hears everything, and that he never forgets, that hereafter he will give every man a spirit-home according to his deserts: If he has been a good man, he will have a good home; if he has been a bad man, he will have a bad home.

This I believe, and all my people believe the same.

Chief Joseph
Nez Perce

The true Indian sets no price upon either his property or his labor. His generosity is limited only by his strength and ability. He regards it as an honor to be selected for a difficult or dangerous service, and would think it shameful to ask for any reward, saying rather: "Let the person I serve express his thanks according to his own bringing up and his sense of honor."

Charles Alexander Eastman (Ohiyesa)
Santee Sioux

Praise, flattery, exaggerated manners, and fine, high-sounding words were no part of Lakota politeness. Excessive manners were put down as insincere, and the constant talker was considered rude and thoughtless. Conversation was never begun at once, or in a hurried manner.

No one was quick with a question, no matter

how important, and no one was pressed for an answer. A pause giving time for thought was the truly courteous way of beginning and conducting a conversation.

Chief Luther Standing Bear
Teton Sioux

This is a happy season of the year—having plenty of provisions, such as beans, squashes, and other produce, with our dried meat and fish. We continue to make feasts and visit each other, until our corn is ripe.

At least one of the lodges in the village makes a feast daily for the Great Spirit. I cannot explain this so that the white people will comprehend me, because we have no regular standard among us. Everyone makes his feast as he thinks best, to please the Great Spirit, who has the care of all beings created.

Black Hawk
Sauk

When you begin a great work you can't expect to finish it all at once; therefore do you and your brothers press on, and let nothing discourage you till you have entirely finished what you have begun.

Now, Brother, as for me, I assure you I will press on, and the contrary winds may blow strong in my face, yet I will go forward and never turn back, and continue to press forward until I have finished, and I would have you do the same. . . .

Though you may hear birds singing on this side and that side, you must not take notice of that, but hear me when I speak to you, and take it to heart, for you may always depend that what I say shall be true.

Teedyuscung
Delaware

My young men shall never farm. Men who work the soil cannot dream, and wisdom comes to us in dreams.

Wowoka
(member of a non-agricultural tribe in Nevada)

If you ever get married, my son, do not make an idol of your wife. The more you worship her, the more she will want to be worshipped. . . . My son, this also I will tell you: Women should never be watched too closely. If you try to watch them, you will merely show your jealousy and become so jealous of your wife that she will leave you and run away. You yourself will be to blame for this.

Anonymous
Winnebago

During the first year a newly married couple discovers whether they can agree with each other and can be happy—if not, they part, and look for other partners. If we were to live together and disagree, we should be as foolish as the whites.

No indiscretion can banish a woman from her parental lodge. It makes no difference how many children she may bring home; she is always welcome. The kettle is over the fire to feed them.

Black Hawk
Sauk

Grandfather says that when your friends die you must not cry. You must not hurt anybody or do harm to anyone. You must not fight. Do right always. It will give you satisfaction in life.

Wovoka
Paiute

If the white man wants to live in peace with the Indian, he can live in peace. Treat all men alike. Give them all the same law. Give them all an even chance to live and grow.

All men were made by the same Great Spirit Chief. They are all brothers. The earth is the mother of all people, and all people should have equal rights upon it. You might as well expect the rivers to run backward as that any man who was born a free man should be contented when penned up and denied liberty to go where he pleases.

If you tie a horse to a stake, do you expect he will grow fat? If you pen an Indian up on a small spot of earth, and compel him to stay there, he will not be contented, nor will he grow and prosper.

Chief Joseph
Nez Perce

We are all poor because we are all honest.

Red Dog
Oglala Sioux

5

The Ways of Leading Others

"No person among us desires any other reward for performing a brave and worthy action, but the consciousness of having served his nation."

Joseph Brant (Thayendanegea)
Mohawk

Something is wrong with the white man's council. When the Micmac people used to have council, the old men would speak and tell the young men what to do—and the young men would listen and do what old men told them to. The white men have changed that, too: Now the young men speak, and the old men listen. I believe the Micmac Council was far better.

Peter Paul (1865)

Why should you take by force from us that which you can obtain by love? Why should you destroy us who have provided you with food? What can you get by war?

It is better to eat good meat, be well, and sleep quietly with my women and children; to laugh and be merry with the English, and be their friend; to have copper hatchets and whatever else I want.

King Wahunsonacook
Powhatan

We now crown you with the sacred emblem of the deer's antlers, the emblem of your Lordship. You shall now become a mentor of the people of the Five Nations. The thickness of your skin shall be seven spans—which is to say that you shall be filled with peace and goodwill and your mind filled with a yearning for the welfare of the people of the Confederacy.

With endless patience you shall carry out your duty, and your firmness shall be tempered with tenderness for your people. Neither anger nor fury shall lodge in your mind, and all your words and actions shall be marked with calm deliberation.

In all your deliberations in the Council, in your efforts at lawmaking, in all your official acts, self-interest shall be cast into oblivion. Cast not away the warnings of any others, if they should chide you for any error or wrong you may do, but return to the way of the Great Law, which is just and right.

Look and listen for the welfare of the whole people and have always in view not only the present but also the coming generations, even those whose faces are yet beneath the surface of the earth—the unborn of the future Nation.

Constitution of the Five Nations

The Onondaga [Iroquois] lords shall open each council by greeting their cousin lords, and expressing their gratitude to them. And they shall offer thanks to the earth where all people dwell—

To the streams of water, the pools, the springs, and the lakes; to the maize and the fruits—

To the medicinal herbs and the trees, to the forest trees for their usefulness, to the animals that serve as food and who offer their pelts as clothing—

To the great winds and the lesser winds; to the Thunderers; and the Sun, the mighty warrior; to the moon—

To the messengers of the Great Spirit who dwells in the skies above, who gives all things useful to men, who is the source and the ruler of health and life.

Then shall the Onondaga lords declare the council open.

Iroquois Constitution

Should any man of the Nation assist with special ability or show great interest in the affairs of the Nation, if he proves himself wise, honest, and worthy of confidence, the Confederate Lords may elect him to a seat with them and he may sit in the Confederate Council. He shall be proclaimed a Pine Tree sprung up for the Nation and be installed as such at the next assembly for the installation of Lords.

Should he ever do anything contrary to the rules of the Great Peace, he may not be deposed from office—no one shall cut him down—but thereafter everyone shall be deaf to his voice and his advice. Should he resign his seat and title, no one shall prevent him. A Pine Tree Chief has no authority to name a successor, nor is his title hereditary.

Constitution of the Five Nations

Try to do something for your people—something difficult. Have pity on your people and love them. If a man is poor, help him. Give him and his family food, give them whatever they ask for. If there is discord among your people, intercede.

Take your sacred pipe and walk into their midst. Die if necessary in your attempt to bring about reconciliation. Then, when order has been restored and they see you lying dead on the ground, still holding in your hand the sacred pipe, the symbol of peace and reconciliation, then assuredly will they know that you have been a real chief.

Winnebago lesson

No person among us desires any other reward for performing a brave and worthy action, but the consciousness of having served his nation.

Joseph Brant (Thayendanegea)
Mohawk

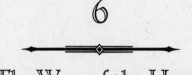

6

The Ways of the Heart

"My friends, how desperately do we need to be loved and to love."

Chief Dan George

My friends, how desperately do we need to be loved and to love. When Christ said that man does not live by bread alone, he spoke of a hunger. This hunger was not the hunger of the body. It was not the hunger for bread. He spoke of a hunger that begins deep down in the very depths of our being. He spoke of a need as vital as breath. He spoke of our hunger for love.

Love is something you and I must have. We must have it because our spirit feeds upon it. We must have it because without it we become weak and faint. Without love our self-esteem weakens. Without it our courage fails. Without love we can no longer look out confidently at the world. We turn inward and begin to feed upon our own personalities, and little by little we destroy ourselves.

With it we are creative. With it we march tirelessly. With it, and with it alone, we are able to sacrifice for others.

Chief Dan George

My heart is filled with joy, when I see you here, as the brooks fill with water when the snows melt in the spring, and I feel glad, as the ponies are when the fresh grass starts in the beginning of the year.

I heard of your coming, when I was many sleeps away, and I made but few camps before I met you. I knew that you had come to do good to me and to my people. I look for the benefits, which would last forever, and so my face shines with joy, as I look upon you.

Ten Bears
Yamparika Comanche

My heart laughs with joy because I am in your presence. . . . Ah, how much more beautiful is the sun today than when you were angry with us!

Chitmachas Chief
(name unknown)

Oh, the comfort, the inexpressible comfort of feeling safe with a person, having neither to weigh thought nor measure words, but pouring them all right out, just as they are, chaff and grain together, certain that a faithful hand will take and sift them, keep what is worth keeping, and with a breath of kindness, blow the rest away.

Anonymous
Shoshone

If all would talk and then do as you have done, the sun of peace would shine forever.

Satank
Kiowa

Friendship is held to be the severest test of character. It is easy, we think, to be loyal to family and

clan, whose blood is in our own veins. Love between man and woman is founded on the mating
instinct and is not free from desire and self-
seeking. But to have a friend, and to be true under
any and all trials, is the mark of a man!

Charles Alexander Eastman (Ohiyesa)
Santee Sioux

Father, I love your daughter, will you give her to
me, that the small roots of her heart may entangle
with mine, so that the strongest wind that blows
shall never separate them.

It is true I love him only, whose heart is like the
sweet juice that runs from the sugar-tree and is
brother to the aspen leaf, that always lives and
shivers.

Anonymous
Canadian

7

The Ways of Believing

"We do not want churches because they will teach us to quarrel about God. . . ."

Chief Joseph
Nez Perce

You tell us that baptism is absolutely necessary to go to heaven. If there were a man so good that he had never offended God, and if he died without baptism, would he go to hell, never having given any offense to God? If he goes to hell, then God must not love all good people, since He throws one into the fire.

You teach us that God existed before the creation of heaven and earth. If He did, where did He live, since there was neither heaven nor earth?

You say that the angels were created in the beginning of the world, and that those who disobeyed were cast into hell. How can that be so, since you say the angels sinned before earth's creation, and hell is in the depths of the earth?

You declare that those who go to hell do not come out of it, and yet you relate stories of the damned who have appeared in the world—how is that to be understood?

Ah, how I would like to kill devils, since they do so much harm! But if they are made like men and some are even among men, do they still feel the fire of hell? Why is it that they do not repent for having offended God? If they did repent, would not God be merciful to them? If Our Lord has suffered for all sinners, why do not they receive pardon from him?

You say that the virgin, mother of Jesus Christ, is not God, and that she has never offended God. You also say that her Son has redeemed all men, and atoned for all; but if she has done nothing wrong, her Son could not redeem her nor atone for her.

Young "savage" seminarians, 12–15 years old,
to the Jesuit father Paul Le Jeune, late 1630s

Our wise men are called Fathers, and they truly sustain that character. Do you call yourselves

Christians? Does then the religion of Him whom you call your Savior inspire your spirit, and guide your practices? Surely not.

It is recorded of him that a bruised reed he never broke. Cease, then, to call yourselves Christians, lest you declare to the world your hypocrisy. Cease, too, to call other nations savage, when you are tenfold more the children of cruelty than they.

Joseph Brant (Thayendanegea)
Mohawk ·

Brother! We are told that you have been preaching to the white people in this place. These people are our neighbors. We are acquainted with them. We will wait a little while, and see what effect your preaching has upon them. If we find it does them good and makes them honest and less disposed to cheat us, we will then consider again becoming Christians.

Red Jacket
Seneca

We have men among us, like the whites, who pretend to know the right path, but will not consent to show it without pay! I have no faith in their paths, but believe that every man must make his own path!

Black Hawk
Sauk

We do not want churches because they will teach us to quarrel about God, as the Catholics and Protestants do. We do not want to learn that.

We may quarrel with men sometimes about things on this earth. But we never quarrel about God. We do not want to learn that.

Chief Joseph
Nez Perce

I think that wherever the Great Spirit places his people, they ought to be satisfied to remain, and thankful for what He has given them, and not drive others from the country He has given them because it happens to be better than theirs!

This is contrary to our way of thinking; and from my intercourse with the whites, I have learned that one great principle of their religion is "to do unto others as you wish them to do unto you!" The settlers on our frontiers and on our lands never seem to think of it, if we are to judge by their actions.

For my part, I am of the opinion that so far as we have reason, we have a right to use it in determining what is right or wrong, and we should pursue that path we believe to be right.

If the Great and Good Spirit wished us to believe and do as the whites, he could easily change our opinions, so that we would see, and think, and act as they do. We are nothing compared to His power, and we feel and know it.

Black Hawk
Sauk

From Wakan Tanka, the Great Spirit, there came a great unifying life force that flowed in and through all things—the flowers of the plains, blowing winds, rocks, trees, birds, animals—and was the same force that had been breathed into the first man. Thus all things were kindred, and were brought together by the same Great Mystery.

Kinship with all creatures of the earth, sky, and water was a real and active principle. In the animal and bird world there existed a brotherly feeling that kept the Lakota safe among them. And so close did some of the Lakotas come to their feathered and furred friends that in true brother-hood they spoke a common tongue.

The animals had rights—the right of man's protection, the right to live, the right to multiply, the right to freedom, and the right to man's in-debtedness—and in recognition of these rights the Lakota never enslaved an animal, and spared all life that was not needed for food and clothing.

This concept of life and its relations was hu-manizing, and gave to the Lakota an abiding love. It filled his being with the joy and mystery of liv-ing; it gave him reverence for all life; it made a place for all things in the scheme of existence with equal importance to all.

The Lakota could despise no creature, for all were of one blood, made by the same hand, and filled with the essence of the Great Mystery. In spirit, the Lakota were humble and meek. "Blessed are the meek, for they shall inherit the earth"—this was true for the Lakota, and from the earth they inherited secrets long since forgotten. Their religion was sane, natural, and human.

Chief Luther Standing Bear
Teton Sioux

Whenever, in the course of the daily hunt, the hunter comes upon a scene that is strikingly beautiful, or sublime—a black thundercloud with the rainbow's glowing arch above the mountain, a white waterfall in the heart of a green gorge, a vast prairie tinged with the blood-red of the sunset—he pauses for an instant in the attitude of worship.

He sees no need for setting apart one day in seven as a holy day, because to him all days are God's days.

Charles Alexander Eastman (Ohiyesa)
Santee Sioux

Grandfather, Great Spirit, once more behold me on earth and lean to hear my feeble voice. You lived first, and you are older than all need, older than all prayer. All things belong to you—the two-legged, the four-legged, the wings of the air, and all green things that live.

You have set the powers of the four quarters of the earth to cross each other. You have made me cross the good road, and the road of difficulties, and where they cross, the place is holy. Day in, day out, forevermore, you are the life of things.

Black Elk
Oglala Sioux

8

The Betrayal of the Land

*"Sell a country! Why not sell the air, the great sea,
as well as the earth?"*

*Tecumseh
Shawnee*

Nothing the Great Mystery placed in the land of
the Indian pleased the white man, and nothing es-
caped his transforming hand. Wherever forests
have not been mowed down, wherever the animal
is recessed in their quiet protection, wherever the
earth is not bereft of four-footed life—that to him
is an "unbroken wilderness."

But, because for the Lakota there was no wilderness, because nature was not dangerous but
hospitable, not forbidding but friendly, Lakota philosophy was healthy—free from fear and dogma-
tism. And here I find the great distinction between
the faith of the Indian and the white man. Indian
faith sought the harmony of man with his sur-

roundings; the other sought the dominance of surroundings.

In sharing, in loving all and everything, one people naturally found a due portion of the thing they sought, while, in fearing, the other found need of conquest.

For one man the world was full of beauty; for the other it was a place of sin and ugliness to be endured until he went to another world, there to become a creature of wings, half-man and half-bird.

Forever one man directed his Mystery to change the world He had made; forever this man pleaded with Him to chastise his wicked ones; and forever he implored his God to send His light to earth. Small wonder this man could not understand the other.

But the old Lakota was wise. He knew that man's heart, away from nature, becomes hard; he knew that lack of respect for growing, living things soon led to lack of respect for humans, too. So he kept his children close to nature's softening influence.

Chief Luther Standing Bear
Oglala Sioux

Some of our chiefs make the claim that the land belongs to us. It is not what the Great Spirit told me. He told me that the lands belong to Him, that no people owns the land; that I was not to forget to tell this to the white people when I met them in council.

Kanekuk
Kickapoo prophet

No tribe has the right to sell, even to each other, much less to strangers. . . . Sell a country! Why not sell the air, the great sea, as well as the earth? Didn't the Great Spirit make them all for the use of his children?

Tecumseh
Shawnee

This is what was spoken by my great-grandfather at the house he made for us. . . . And these are the words that were given him by the Master of Life: "At some time there shall come among you a stranger, speaking a language you do not understand. He will try to buy the land from you, but do not sell it; keep it for an inheritance to your children."

Aseenewub
Red Lake Ojibwe

My reason teaches me that land cannot be sold. The Great Spirit gave it to his children to live upon and cultivate as far as necessary for their subsistence, and so long as they occupy and cultivate it they have the right to the soil, but if they voluntarily leave it then any other people have a right to settle on it. Nothing can be sold, except things that can be carried away.

Black Hawk
Sauk

Suppose a white man should come to me and say, "Joseph, I like your horses. I want to buy them."

I say to him, "No, my horses suit me; I will not sell them."

Then he goes to my neighbor and says to him, "Joseph has some good horses. I want to buy them, but he refuses to sell."

My neighbor answers, "Pay me the money and I will sell you Joseph's horses."

The white man returns to me and says, "Joseph, I have bought your horses and you must let me have them."

If we sold our lands to the government, this is the way they bought them.

Chief Joseph
Nez Perce

We know our lands have now become more valuable. The white people think we do not know their value; but we know that the land is everlasting, and the few goods we receive for it are soon worn out and gone.

Canassatego
Treaty negotiations with Six Nations

On this land there is a great deal of timber, pine and oak, that are of much use to the white man. They send it to foreign countries, and it brings them a great deal of money.

On the land there is much grass for cattle and horses, and much good food for hogs.

On this land there is a great deal of tobacco raised, which likewise brings much money. Even the streams are valuable to the white man, to grind the wheat and corn that grows on this land. The pine trees that are dead are valuable for tar.

All these things are lasting benefits. But if the Indians are given just a few goods for their lands, in one or two seasons those goods are all rotted and gone for nothing.

We are told that our lands are of no service to us; but still, if we hold our lands, there will always be a turkey, or a deer, or a fish in the streams for those young who will come after us.

We are afraid if we part with any more of our lands the white people will not let us keep as much as will be sufficient to bury our dead.

Doublehead
Creek Chief

My friends, when I went to Washington I went into your money-house and I had some young men with me, but none of us took any money out of that house. At the same time, when your Great Father's people come into my country, they go into my money-house and take money out.

Long Mandan
Sioux

In early life, I was deeply hurt as I witnessed the grand old forests of Michigan, under whose shades my forefathers lived and died, falling before the cyclone of civilization as before a prairie fire.

In those days, I traveled thousands of miles along our winding trails, through the unbroken solitudes of the wild forest, listening to the songs of the woodland birds as they poured forth their melodies from the thick foliage above and about me.

Very seldom now do I catch one familiar note from these early warblers of the woods. They have all passed away. . . .

I now listen to the songs of other birds that have come with the advance of civilization . . . and, like the wildwood birds our fathers used to hold their breath to hear, they sing in concert, without pride, without envy, without jealousy— alike in forest and field, alike before wigwam or castle, alike before savage or sage, alike for chief or king.

Simon Pokagon
Potawatomi Chief

We know that the white man does not understand our ways. One portion of the land is the same to him as the next, for he is a stranger who comes in the night and takes from the land whatever he needs. The earth is not his brother, but his en- emy—and when he has conquered it, he moves on. He leaves his fathers' graves, and his children's birthright is forgotten.

Chief Seattle
Suqwamish and Duwamish

9

The Ways of Dying

"Death will come, always out of season."

Big Elk
Omaha Chief

I was born upon the prairie where the wind blew
free and there was nothing to break the light of the
sun. I was born where there were no enclosures
and where everything drew a free breath.

I want to die there, and not within walls.

Ten Bears
Yamparika Comanche

When an infant dies before its fourth day of life,
mourning shall continue only five days.

Then shall you gather the little boys and girls
at the house of mourning, and at the funeral feast
a speaker shall address the children and bid them

be happy once more, even though by a death, gloom has been cast over them.

Then shall the black clouds roll away and the sky shall show blue once more. Then shall the children be again in sunshine.

Constitution of the Five Nations

If my warriors are to fight they are too few; if they are to die they are too many.

Hendrick
Mohawk

What! Would you wish that there should be no dried trees in the woods and no dead branches on a tree that is growing old?

A seventy-year-old Huron

Do not grieve. Misfortunes will happen to the wisest and best of men. Death will come, always out of season. It is the command of the Great Spirit, and all nations and people must obey. What is past and what cannot be prevented should not be grieved for. . . . Misfortunes do not flourish particularly in our lives—they grow everywhere.

Big Elk
Omaha Chief

Old age was simply a delightful time, when the old people sat on the sunny doorsteps, playing in the sun with the children, until they fell asleep. At last, they failed to wake up.

James Paytiamo
Acoma Pueblo

Each soul must meet the morning sun, the new, sweet earth, and the Great Silence alone!

Charles Alexander Eastman (Ohiyesa)
Santee Sioux

10

The Passing of the Ways

"Our Indian life, I know, is gone forever."

Waheenee
Hidatsa (North Dakota)

When I was a boy, the Sioux owned the world. The sun rose and set on their land; they sent ten thousand men to battle.

Where are the warriors today? Who slew them? Where are our lands? Who owns them?

What white man can say I ever stole his land or a penny of his money? Yet they say I am a thief.

What white woman, however lonely, was ever captive or insulted by me? Yet they say I am a bad Indian.

What white man has ever seen me drunk? Who has ever come to me hungry and left me unfed? Who has ever seen me beat my wives or abuse my children? What law have I broken?

Is it wrong for me to love my own? Is it wicked for me because my skin is red? Because I am a Sioux? Because I was born where my father lived? Because I would die for my people and my country?

Sitting Bull
Teton Sioux

The ground on which we stand is sacred ground. It is the dust and blood of our ancestors. On these plains the Great White Father in Washington sent his soldiers armed with long knives and rifles to slay the Indian. Many of them sleep on yonder hill where Pahaska—White Chief of the Long Hair [General Custer]—so bravely fought and fell.

A few more passing suns will see us here no more, and our dust and bones will mingle with these same prairies. I see as in a vision the dying spark of our council fires, the ashes cold and white. I see no longer the curling smoke rising from our lodge poles. I hear no longer the songs of the women as they prepare the meal.

The antelope have gone; the buffalo wallows are empty. Only the wail of the coyote is heard. The white man's medicine is stronger than ours; his iron horse [the railroad] rushes over the buffalo trail. He talks to us through his "whispering spirit" [the telephone].

We are like birds with a broken wing. My heart is cold within me. My eyes are growing dim—I am old.

Chief Plenty Coups
Crow

As a child, I understood how to give; I have forgotten that grace since I became civilized. I lived the natural life, whereas I now live the artificial. Any pretty pebble was valuable to me then, every growing tree an object of reverence.

Now I worship with the white man before a painted landscape whose value is estimated in dollars! Thus the Indian is reconstructed, as the natural rocks are ground to powder and made into artificial blocks that may be built into the walls of modern society.

Charles Alexander Eastman (Ohiyesa)
Santee Sioux

When the buffalo went away the hearts of my people fell to the ground, and they could not lift them up again.

After this nothing happened. There was little singing anywhere.

Chief Plenty Coups
Crow

I remember the old men of my village. These old, old men used to prophesy about the coming of the white man. They would go about tapping their canes on the adobe floor of the house, and call to us children.

"Listen! Listen! The gray-eyed people are coming nearer and nearer. They are building an iron road. They are coming nearer every day. There will be a time when you will mix with these people. That is when the Gray Eyes are going to get you to drink hot, black water, which you will drink whenever you eat. Then your teeth will become soft.

"They will get you to smoke at a young age, so that your eyes will run tears on windy days, and your eyesight will be poor. Your joints will crack when you want to move slowly and softly.

"You will sleep on soft beds and will not like to rise early. When you begin to wear heavy clothes and sleep under heavy covers, then you will grow lazy. Then there will be no more singing heard in the valleys as you walk.

"When you begin to eat with iron sticks, your tones will grow louder. You will speak louder and talk over your parents. You will grow disobedient. You will mix with those gray-eyed people, and you will learn their ways; you will break up your homes, and murder and steal."

Such things have come true, and I have to compare my generation with the old generation. We are not as good as they were; we are not as healthy as they were.

How did these old men know what was coming? That is what I would like to know.

James Paytiamo
Acoma Pueblo

I am an old woman now. The buffaloes and black-tail deer are gone, and our Indian ways are almost gone. Sometimes I find it hard to believe that I ever lived them.

My little son grew up in the white man's school. He can read books, and he owns cattle and has a farm. He is a leader among our Hidatsa people, helping teach them to follow the white man's road.

He is kind to me. We no longer live in an earth lodge, but in a house with chimneys, and my son's wife cooks by a stove.

But for me, I cannot forget our old ways.

Often in summer I rise at daybreak and steal out to the corn fields, and as I hoe the corn I sing to it, as we did when I was young. No one cares for our corn songs now.

Sometimes in the evening I sit, looking out on the big Missouri. The sun sets, and dusk steals over the water. In the shadows I seem again to see our Indian village, with smoke curling upward from the earth lodges, and in the river's roar I hear the yells of the warriors, and the laughter of little children as of old.

It is but an old woman's dream. Then I see but shadows and hear only the roar of the river, and tears come into my eyes. Our Indian life, I know, is gone forever.

Waheenee
Hidatsa (North Dakota)

11

---◆---

The Ways of the White Man

"What do we know of the manner of the laws and customs of the white people?"

> *Black Hawk*
> *Sauk*

Many of the white man's ways are past our understanding. . . . They put a great store upon writing; there is always a paper.

The white people must think paper has some mysterious power to help them in the world. The Indian needs no writings; words that are true sink deep into his heart, where they remain. He never forgets them. On the other hand, if the white man loses his papers, he is helpless.

I once heard one of their preachers say that no white man was admitted to heaven unless there were writings about him in a great book!

Four Guns
Oglala Sioux

I am truly astonished that the French have so little cleverness. They try to persuade us to convert our poles, our barks, and our wigwams into their houses of stone and of wood that are as tall and lofty as these trees. Very well! But why do men of five to six feet in height need houses that are sixty to eighty?

Do we not have all the advantages in our houses that you have in yours, such as reposing, drinking, sleeping, eating, and amusing ourselves with our friends when we wish?

Have you as much ingenuity as the Indians, who carry their houses and their wigwams with them so that they may lodge wherever they please? We can say that we are at home every-where, because we set up our wigwams with ease wherever we go, without asking permission from anyone.

You reproach us—very inappropriately—and tell us that our country is a little hell in contrast with France, which you compare to a terrestrial paradise. If this is true, why did you leave it? Why did you abandon your wives, children, relatives, and friends?

Which of these is the wisest and happiest—he who labors without ceasing and only obtains, with great trouble, enough to live on, or he who rests in comfort and finds all that he needs in the pleasure of hunting and fishing?

Learn now, my brother, once and for all, because I must open my heart to you: There is no Indian who does not consider himself infinitely more happy and more powerful than the French.

Micmac Chief (1676)

The English, in general, are a noble, generous-minded people, free to act and free to think. They very much pride themselves on their civil and religious privileges; on their learning, generosity, manufacturing, and commerce; and they think that no other nation is equal to them. . . .

No nation, I think, can be more fond of novelties than the English; they gaze upon foreigners as if they had just dropped down from the moon. . . .

They are truly industrious, and in general

very honest and upright. But their close attention to business produces, I think, too much worldly-mindedness, and hence they forget to think enough about their souls and their God.

Their motto seems to be "Money, money, get money, get rich, and be a gentleman." With this sentiment, they fly about in every direction, like a swarm of bees, in search of the treasure that lies so near their hearts.

Peter Jones, or Kahkewaquonaby
("Sacred Waving Feathers")
Ojibwe

Once I was in Victoria, and I saw a very large house. They told me it was a bank, and that the white men place their money there to be taken care of, and that by and by they got it back, with interest.

We are Indians, and we have no such bank; but when we have plenty of money or blankets, we give them away to other chiefs and people, and by and by they return them, with interest, and our hearts feel good. Our way of giving is our bank.

Maquinna
Nootka Chief

Strong liquor was first sold to us by the Dutch, and they were blind, they had no eyes, they could not see how much it hurt us. The next people who came were the Swedes, who continued to sell us strong liquor. We love it, so we cannot refuse it.

It makes us wild; we do not know what we are doing. We abuse one another; we throw one another into the fire. . . .

Through drinking, seven score of our people have been killed. The cask must be sealed, it must be made fast; it must not leak by day or night, in the light or in the dark.

Okanicon
Delaware

The Americans have been very kind to us; they are not as arrogant as the English, but very persevering in all their ways.

They pay more respect to their women than the English, and they see the things that belong to others without bitterness, or regret. The working classes of the English call their rich men "Big Bugs," but the Yankees call them "Top Notches."

The Yankees put their feet upon the tables, chairs, or chimney pieces when smoking their cigars or reading their newspapers. They are not as much slaves to their civilization as the English; they like to be comfortable, something like ourselves, placing one leg upon the other knee while basking ourselves in the sun.

A real comfort is better than an artificial one to the human nature.

George Henry
Maungwudaus ("Big Legging")
Ojibwe Methodist preacher

I have attended dinners among white people. Their ways are not our ways.

We eat in silence, quietly smoke a pipe, and depart. Thus is our host honored.

This is not the way of the white man. After his food has been eaten, one is expected to say foolish things. Then the host feels honored.

Four Guns
Oglala Sioux

They are a heartless nation, that is certain. They have made some of their people servants—yes, slaves! We have never believed in keeping slaves, but it seems that the white people do! It is our belief that they painted their servants black a long time ago, to tell them from the rest—and now the slaves have children born to them of the same color!

The greatest object of their lives seems to be to acquire possessions—to be rich. They desire to possess the whole world.

For thirty years they tried to entice us to sell our land to them. Finally, their soldiers took it by force, and we have been driven away from our beautiful country.

They are indeed an extraordinary people. They have divided the day into hours, like the moons of the year. In fact, they measure everything. Not one of them would let so much as a turnip go from his field unless he received full value for it. I understand that sometimes their great men make a feast and invite many, but when it is over, the guests are required to pay for what they have eaten before leaving the house. . . .

I am also told, but this I hardly believe, that their Great Chief compels every man to pay him for the land he lives upon and all his personal goods—even those he needs for his own existence—every year. I am sure we could not live under such a law.

In war they have leaders and war-chiefs of different grades. The common warriors are driven forward like a herd of antelopes to face the foe. It is because of this manner of fighting—from compulsion and not from personal bravery—that we count no coup on them. A lone warrior can do much harm to a large army of them—especially when they are in unfamiliar territory.

Charles Alexander Eastman's uncle
Santee Sioux

The white man who is our agent is so stingy that he carries a linen rag in his pocket into which to blow his nose, for fear he might blow away something of value.

Piapot
Cree Chief

I have carried a heavy load on my back ever since I was a boy. I realized then that we could not hold our own with the white men. We were like deer. They were like grizzly bears. We had a small country. Their country was large. We were contented to let things remain as the Great Spirit Chief made them. They were not, and would change the rivers and mountains if they did not suit them.

Chief Joseph
Nez Perce

Here, for the first time, I touched the goose quill to the treaty—not knowing, however, that by that act I consented to give away my village! Had that been explained to me, I should have opposed it, and never would have signed their treaty, as my recent conduct has clearly proven.

What do we know of the manner of the laws and customs of the white people? They might buy our bodies for dissection, and we would touch the goose quill to confirm it, without knowing what we were doing. This was the case with myself and my people in touching the goose quill the first time.

We can only judge what is proper and right by our standard of right and wrong, which differs widely from the whites, if I have been correctly informed. The whites may do bad all their lives, and then, if they are sorry for it when they are about to die, all is well!

But with us it is different: We must continue throughout our lives to do what we conceive to be good. If we have corn and meat, and know of a family that has none, we divide with them. If we have more blankets than are sufficient, and others have not enough, we must give to them that want.

Black Hawk
Sauk

Brothers, money to us is of no value, and to most of us unknown; and as no consideration whatever can induce us to sell the lands, on which we get sustenance for our women and children, we hope we may be allowed to point out a mode by which your settlers may be easily removed and peace obtained.

Brothers, we know that these settlers are poor, or they would never have ventured to live in a country that has been in continual trouble ever since they crossed the Ohio. Divide therefore this large sum of money that you have offered to us among these people . . . and we are persuaded they would most readily accept it in lieu of the lands you sold to them. . . .

Letter (1793)
The Seven Nations of Canada

Tell your people that since the Great Father promised that we should never be removed we have been moved five times. I think you had better put the Indians on wheels so you can run them about wherever you wish.

Anonymous Chief (1876)

I know that robes, leggings, moccasins, bear claws, and so on are of little value to you, but we wish you to have them and to preserve them in some conspicuous part of your lodge, so that when we are gone and the sod turned over our bones, if our children should visit this place, as we do now, they may see and recognize with pleasure the things of their fathers, and reflect on the times that are past.

Sharitarish
Pawnee

I will follow the white man's trail. I will make him my friend, but I will not bend my back to his burdens. I will be cunning as a coyote. I will ask him to help me understand his ways, then I will prepare the way for my children. Maybe they will outrun the white man in his own shoes.

There are but two ways for us. One leads to

hunger and death, the other leads to where the poor white man lives. Beyond is the happy hunting ground where the white man cannot go.

Many Horses
Oglala Sioux

12

The Ways of Civilization

"Civilization has been thrust upon me . . . and it has not added one whit to my love for truth, honesty, and generosity. . . ."

Chief Luther Standing Bear
Oglala Sioux

Much has been said of the want of what you term "civilization" among the Indians. Many proposals have been made to us to adopt your laws, your religion, your manners, and your customs. We do not see the propriety of such a reformation.

We should be better pleased if we could actually see the good effects of these doctrines in your own practices rather than hearing you talk about them, or reading your newspapers on such subjects.

You say, for example, "Why do not the Indians till the ground and live as we do?" May we not ask with equal propriety, "Why do not the white people hunt and live as we do?"

Old Tassel
Cherokee

The more I consider the condition of the white men, the more fixed becomes my opinion that, instead of gaining, they have lost much by subjecting themselves to what they call the laws and regulations of civilized societies.

Tomochichi
Creek Chief

In the government you call civilized, the happiness of the people is constantly sacrificed to the splendor of empire. Hence the origin of your codes of criminal and civil laws; hence your dungeons and prisons. We have no prisons; we have no pompous parade of courts; we have no written laws; and yet judges are as highly revered among us as they are among you, and their decisions are as much regarded.

We have among us no exalted villains above

the control of our laws. Daring wickedness is here never allowed to triumph over helpless innocence. The estates of widows and orphans are never devoured by enterprising swindlers.

We have no robbery under the pretext of law.

Joseph Brant (Thayendanegea)
Mohawk

The white man's police have protected us only as well as the feathers of a bird protect it from the frosts of winter.

Crowfoot
Blackfeet Chief

The sight of your cities pains the eyes of the red man. But perhaps it is because the red man is a savage and does not understand.

There is no quiet place in the white man's cities, no place to hear the leaves of spring or the rustle of insects' wings. Perhaps it is because I am a savage and do not understand, but the clatter only seems to insult the ears.

The Indian prefers the soft sound of the wind darting over the face of the pond, the smell of the wind itself cleansed by a midday rain, or scented with pinon pine. The air is precious to the red man, for all things share the same breath—the animals, the trees, the man.

Like a man who has been dying for many days, a man in your city is numb to the stench.

Chief Seattle
Suqwamish and Duwamish

The Great Spirit has given the white man great foresightedness; he sees everything at a distance, and his mind invents and makes the most extraordinary things. But the red man has been made shortsighted. He sees only what is close around him and knows nothing except what his father knew. . . .

Crow Belly
Gros Ventre Chief

The attempted transformation of the Indian by the white man and the chaos that has resulted are but the fruits of the white man's disobedience of a fundamental and spiritual law.

"Civilization" has been thrust upon me since the days of the reservations, and it has not added one whit to my sense of justice, to my reverence for the rights of life, to my love for truth, honesty, and generosity, or to my faith in Wakan Tanka, God of the Lakotas.

For after all the great religions have been preached and expounded, or have been revealed by brilliant scholars, or have been written in fine books and embellished in fine language with finer covers, man—all man—is still confronted with the Great Mystery.

Chief Luther Standing Bear
Oglala Sioux

White man's pictures all fade, but the Indian's memories last forever.

Indian guide to Tom Wilson (1882)

13

---◆---

Heed These Words

"Continue to contaminate your own bed, and you will one night suffocate in your own waste."

Chief Seattle
Suqwamish and Duwamish

The white man does not understand America. He is too far removed from its formative processes. The roots of the tree of his life have not yet grasped the rock and the soil.

The white man is still troubled by primitive fears; he still has in his consciousness the perils of this frontier continent, some of it not yet having yielded to his questing footsteps and inquiring eyes.

He shudders still with the memory of the loss of his forefathers upon its scorching deserts and forbidding mountaintops. The man from Europe is still a foreigner and an alien. And he still hates the man who questioned his path across the continent.

But in the Indian the spirit of the land is still vested; it will be a long time until other men are able to divine and meet its rhythm. Men must be born and reborn to belong. Their bodies must be formed of the dust of their forefathers' bones.

Chief Luther Standing Bear
Oglala Sioux

A few more hours, a few more winters, and none of the children of the great tribes that once lived on this earth, or that roamed in small bands in the woods, will be left to mourn the graves of a people once as powerful and hopeful as yours.

The whites, too, shall pass—perhaps sooner than other tribes. Continue to contaminate your own bed, and you will one night suffocate in your own waste.

When the buffalo are all slaughtered, the wild horses all tamed, the secret corners of the forest heavy with the scent of many men, and the view of the ripe hills blotted by talking wires, where is the thicket? Gone. Where is the eagle? Gone.

And what is it to say farewell to the swift and

the hunt, to the end of living and the beginning of survival? We might understand if we knew what it was that the white man dreams, what he describes to his children on the long winter nights, what visions he burns into their minds, so they will wish for tomorrow. But we are savages. The white man's dreams are hidden from us.

Chief Seattle
Suqwamish and Duwamish

If the Great Spirit had desired me to be a white man he would have made me so in the first place. He put in your heart certain wishes and plans; in my heart he put other and different desires.

Each man is good in the sight of the Great Spirit. It is not necessary for eagles to be crows. Now we are poor but we are free. No white man controls our footsteps. If we must die, we die defending our rights.

Sitting Bull
Teton Sioux

The white people think we have no brains in our heads. They are great and powerful, and that makes them make war with us. We are but a little handful to what you are.

But remember . . . when you hunt for a rattlesnake, you usually cannot find it—and perhaps it will bite you before you see it.

Shingis
Delaware Chief

The red man has ever fled the approach of the white man, as the morning mist flees before the morning sun. . . . It matters little where we pass the remnants of our days. They will not be many.

But why should I mourn the untimely fate of my people? Your time of decay may be distant, but it will surely come, for even the white man, whose God walked and talked with him as friend with friend, cannot be exempt from the common destiny. We may be brothers, after all. We will see. . . .

Chief Seattle
Suqwamish and Duwamish

I know that my race must change. We cannot hold our own with the white men as we are. We ask only an even chance to live as other men live. We ask to be recognized as men. We ask that the same law shall work alike on all men. If the Indian breaks the law, punish him by the law. If the white man breaks the law, punish him also.

Let me be a free man—free to travel, free to stop, free to work, free to trade where I choose, free to choose my own teachers, free to follow the religion of my fathers, free to think and talk and act for myself—and I will obey every law, or submit to the penalty.

When the white man treats the Indian as the Indians treat each other, then we will have no more wars. We shall all be alike—brothers of one father and one mother, with one sky above us and one country around us, and one government for all. Then the Great Spirit Chief who rules above will smile upon this land, and send rain to wash out the bloody spots from the face of the earth that were made by brothers' hands. For this time the Indian race is waiting and praying.

I hope that no more groans of wounded men and women will ever go to the ear of the Great Spirit Chief above, and that all people may be one people.

Chief Joseph
Nez Perce

Can we talk of integration until there is integration of hearts and minds? Unless you have this, you have only a physical presence, and the walls between us are as high as the mountain range.

Chief Dan George

The color of the skin makes no difference. What is good and just for one is good and just for the other, and the Great Spirit made all men brothers.

I have a red skin, but my grandfather was a white man. What does it matter? It is not the color of the skin that makes me good or bad.

White Shield
Arikara Chief

The path to glory is rough, and many gloomy hours obscure it. May the Great Spirit shed light on your path, so that you may never experience the humility that the power of the American government has reduced me to. This is the wish of a man who, in his native forests, was once as proud and bold as yourself.

Black Hawk
Sauk

Every part of all this soil is sacred to my people. Every hillside, every valley, every plain and grove has been hallowed by some sad or happy event in days long vanished. The very dust you now stand on responds more willingly to their footsteps than to yours, because it is rich with the blood of our ancestors and our bare feet are conscious of the sympathetic touch.

Even the little children who lived here and rejoiced here for a brief season love these somber solitudes, and at eventide they greet shadowy returning spirits.

And when the last red man shall have perished, and the memory of my tribe shall have become a myth among the white men, these shores will swarm with the invisible dead of my tribe; and when our children's children think themselves alone in the field, the store, the shop, upon the highway, or in the silence of the pathless woods, they will not be alone.

At night when the streets of your cities and villages are silent and you think them deserted, they will throng with the returning hosts that once filled and still love this beautiful land.

The white man will never be alone.

Let him be just and deal kindly with my people, for the dead are not powerless. Dead, did

I say? There is no death, only a change of worlds.

Chief Seattle
Suqwamish and Duwamish

Biographical Notes

Aseenewub
Red Lake Ojibwe (19th century)
Also known as Little Rock. He was part of the 1863 treaty negotiations where the U.S. government surrounded the Ojibwe negotiators with cannon and threatened them with hanging if they did not sign over their land.

Big Elk
Omaha Chief (ca. 1772–1846)
A great peacemaker, although he led war parties on the Pawnees. Also a renowned orator. Once painted by George Catlin. Traveled to Washington, D.C., to sign peace treaties.

Black Elk
Oglala Sioux (ca. 1863–1950)
Medicine man and spiritual leader. Witnessed the Battle of Big Horn at the age of thirteen. Once fled to Canada with his family to avoid being sent to a reservation. Had many dreams and mystical ex-

periences. Dictated his life story in the well-known book, *Black Elk Speaks: The Life Story of a Holy Man of the Oglala Sioux.*

Black Hawk
Sauk and Fox Brave (1767–1838)
Black Hawk's mission in life was to right the wrong he saw done in 1804, when William Henry Harrison plied four chiefs of Black Hawk's tribe with drink so they would sign away the Sauk's land. He encouraged the British to make war with the Americans to stop their westward movement. When even the little land his people had saved began to be squatted on by settlers, Black Hawk went to battle. He eventually became a prisoner of war for several months, then was sent home a folk hero of sorts, hailed by non-Indians as a symbol of the old wild west. In a last insult his dead body was desecrated by vandals.

Canassatego
Onondaga (date of birth unknown–1750)
Canassatego represented the Iroquois in negotiations with the British. Probably killed by pro-French Iroquois.

Charles Alexander Eastman (Ohiyesa)
Santee Sioux (1858–1939)
An author and the first native American physi-

cian. He was born in Redwood Falls, Minnesota. Received a B.S. degree from Dartmouth and attended medical school at Boston University. Was instrumental in founding the Boy Scouts of America and the Campfire Girls. Died in Detroit, Michigan.

Chief Dan George
Coast Salish (20th century)
Hereditary chief. Perhaps best known for his role in the movie *Little Big Man*. Tried to use his writings and media roles to give an accurate depiction of American Indian beliefs and values.

Chief Joseph
Nez Perce (1840–1904)
Best known for his extraordinary attempt to lead his tribe through the western Rockies to Canada to escape the approaching U.S. Army. They were desperate to avoid being forced onto reservations. After three months, they were caught, and Joseph lived out his life on a reservation. He visited Washington, D.C., the year before he died.

Chief Luther Standing Bear
Oglala Sioux (1868–1939)
Wished for his people to live a nomadic lifestyle, but tried to accommodate to white ways by attend-

ing Carlisle Indian School and encouraging his people to take up farming. Turned away from white culture after witnessing the slaughter of unarmed men, women, and children at Wounded Knee in 1890. Published a book, *My Indian Boyhood*, in 1933.

Chief Plenty Coups (Aleek-chea-ahoosh)
Crow (1849–1932)
A warrior, but never fought against the white man. Became a chief at only twenty-five years of age. He was one of the first of his people to take up farming and ranching. Was said to have eleven wives, but no children. Willed his land to the American people as a memorial park to the Crow Nation. It is now a museum.

Chief Seattle
Suqwamish and Duwamish (1786–1866)
Seattle was a Christian and an ally of the white man. He agreed to settle the Washington tribes on reservations in 1855. He gave a speech to the governor of Washington Territory in 1853.

Cochise ("Like Ironweed")
Chiricahua Apache Chief
(date of birth unknown–1874)
Originally acquiesced to the white advance across

the Southwest. Turned against the Americans when his people were falsely accused of kidnapping a young boy. Subsequently fought the whites for many years in the Southwest. He and his warriors were legendary for their surprise attacks, uncompromising ruthlessness in pursuit of their own goals, and knowledge of their own land. He died a natural death.

Crow Belly
Gros Ventre Chief (mid-19th century)

Crowfoot
Blackfeet Chief (late 19th century)
Crowfoot was a hunter and warrior who ceded the land of his people to the Canadian government without realizing what he was doing.

Four Guns
Oglala Sioux (late 19th century)
A judge

George Copway (Kahgegagahbowh)
Ojibwe (ca. 1818– ca. 1863)
One of the first Indian writers to be widely read by whites. Born in Ontario to a hereditary chief, and became a missionary. Translated religious texts into Ojibwe.

George Henry
Ojibwe Methodist Preacher

Gertrude S. Bonnin (Zitkala-Sa)
Yankton Sioux (1875–1938)
Teacher, musician and writer. Educated by Quakers, and taught at Carlisle Indian School in Pennsylvania. Wrote articles for *Harper's* and *Atlantic*. Activist in political affairs. Founded Council of American Indians.

Joseph Brant (Thayendanegea)
Mohawk (ca. 1742–1807)
Dedicated his life to the fight for the right of the Five Nations to be free. He was an intellectual, a military strategist, and a translator of religious documents. He was the most famous war chief of the Five Nations in their fight to ward off the advancing Europeans. Later, he decided to fight on the side of the British in the Revolutionary War after a fact-finding mission to England. He was no stranger to Washington, D.C., and it was there that he was known for his eloquence and good sense. He died in battle.

Kanekuk
Kickapoo prophet (ca. 1785–1852)
Tribal chief, religious pacifist. Encouraged farming

among his people and received assistance from the federal government as a result. His people were finally forced off their land by encroaching white settlers. Died of smallpox.

King Hendrick (Tiyanoga)
Mohawk (ca. 1680–1755)
Once met Queen Anne in England, and thereafter was dubbed "King Hendrick." Criticized British army strategy against the French in North America. Died in battle against the French.

King Wahunsonacook
Powhatan
Led a confederacy of thirty-two bands. Had twenty sons and eleven daughters, one of whom was Pocahontas. To gain his support for their settlement at Jamestown, the English placed a gold crown on his head and proclaimed him "King Powhatan."

Long Mandan
Sioux
Opposed the white attempts to take the Black Hills of South Dakota, which the Sioux considered the sacred center of the world.

Many Horses
Oglala Sioux (date of birth unknown–1867)
War chief and wealthy breeder of horses, which he acquired in raids. Killed in battle.

Maquinna
Nootka Chief (early 19th century)
Attacked a trading ship in 1803, and killed the entire crew except for two people. One of the captives wrote an account which was widely read by whites.

Peter Jones
(Kahkewaquonaby or Sacred Waving Feathers)
Ojibwe (1802–1856)
Author of *A History of the Ojhibwe Indian*, still a highly regarded text. An Episcopal minister and a missionary to Eastern Ontario. Traveled extensively, to New York, London, and many other cities.

Red Cloud
Oglala Sioux (ca. 1822–1909)
Red Cloud initially believed that making peace with the white government was the only way to promote an orderly passage of whites through Indian land. But unkept treaty promises prompted him to take up arms and fight the whites in 1866. After humiliating General Sherman with his mil-

itary forays, he again promoted a just peace and led a group called Red Cloud's Peace Crusade to Washington, D.C., in 1870. The government's failure to live up to its promises a second time left him embittered. He remained a spokesman for his people until his death.

Red Dog
Oglala Sioux (19th century)
Red Dog was adamantly opposed to the white miners and settlers who poured into the Black Hills of South Dakota in search of gold. He was an eloquent spokesman for Indian rights who consistently confronted the white government for its betrayal of its treaty obligations.

Red Jacket (Sa-Go-Ye-Wat-Ha)
Seneca (1756–1830)
Red Jacket was a warrior and an orator. He spent several weeks in Washington, D.C., where he met with President George Washington and addressed the U.S. Senate. He was open about his contempt for the white man's religion.

Satank
Kiowa (ca. 1810–1871)
Satank negotiated a peace treaty between the Kiowas and the Cheyennes. However, he was not a

peacemaker with the white man. Though he knew that his people could not drive the whites away, he led raids against the settlers in an attempt to stop their fencing of the land and killing of game. He was eventually captured. Even then, he attacked a guard on his way to prison and was shot to death. His body was thrown in a ditch.

Satanta
Kiowa Chief (ca. 1830–1878)
Sometimes called the "Orator of the Plains." He fought against the westward expansion of the railroads because he knew they would disrupt the buffalo herds that were the basis of Kiowa survival. He was taken prisoner by General Sherman, who tricked him with false claims of a peaceful council meeting. He committed suicide while imprisoned in Texas.

Sharitarish
Pawnee (ca. 1790–1822)
Met Zebulon Pike in Nebraska. Delivered a speech to President Monroe about self-determination. Died of cholera.

Simon Pokagon
Potawatomi Chief (1830–1899)
Lecturer and writer. Educated at Notre Dame. Was

a professional organist and spoke five languages fluently. Met with both President Lincoln and President Grant.

Sitting Bull (Tatanka Yotanka)
Teton Sioux (late 19th century)
A medicine man and tribal chief. He consistently explained to the whites that he did not wish to fight them, but only to hunt on his own land. Eventually the Teton Sioux prevailed upon him to become their war chief when the whites insisted on wantonly killing the buffalo and despoiling grazing lands. He is best known for his defeat of Custer at the Battle of Little Big Horn, and for his endurance in the Sun Dance. He is considered to be the last Sioux to surrender to the U.S. government. He was murdered by tribal police who were sent to arrest him.

Tecumseh
Shawnee (1768–1813)
Tecumseh spent his life trying to convince the Six Nations to ally themselves with the Indians in the Ohio and Mississippi Valleys to stop the white man. He was a highly respected warrior and statesman, and was a commissioned brigadier general in the British armed forces in Canada. He was killed in battle in Ontario.

Teedyuscung
Delaware (ca. 1705–1763)
Tribal chief. Fought to keep his people's land. Converted to Christianity, but later went back to his traditional way of life. Sided with the British against the French. Was a heavy drinker, but still respected. Burned to death in his home as a result of a fire set by a personal enemy.

Ten Bears
Yamparika Comanche (1792–1872)
More a poet than a warrior, he was considered a great peacemaker. He spent his life seeking concessions from Washington and keeping the Comanches from going to war. He was largely unsuccessful, but was admired by everyone for his heroic efforts. He died a bitter man.

Tomochichi
Creek Chief (ca. 1650–1739)
Friendly to colonists. Traveled to England, where he gave numerous speeches. Initiated trade between England and his people.

White Shield
Arikara (Southern Cheyenne) Chief
(ca. 1833–1883)
Peacemaker. Met with President Grant. Opposed

white ranchers being allowed to graze their cattle on his people's lands.

Wovoka
Paiute (late 19th century)
Known as "The Paiute Messiah." Fell ill with a fever during a solar eclipse in 1889 and thereafter had visions. Preached that the Great Spirit would restore Indian people to their former glory if they all participated in the Ghost Dance. The Ghost Dance became a great religious ceremony among the plains Indians in the 1890s.

Additional Notes

Constitution of the Five Nations
The Five Nations of the Cayuga, Mohawk, Oneida, Onondaga, and Seneca formed the Iroquois Confederation long before Columbus set foot on America. They later became known as the Six Nations when the Tuscarora joined the Confederation. Their constitution was used by Benjamin Franklin as a model for the Articles of Confederation.

Treaty negotiations with the Six Nations were in the early to mid-18th century.

The Sioux tribes were sometimes called the Dakota. They originally inhabited the Upper Midwest. They are sometimes divided into three dialect groups, each group consisting of several tribes:

(1) The Dakota are the Santee or Eastern group, composed of the Mdewakanton, Sisseton, Wahpeton, and Wahpehnta tribes.

(2) The Nakota is the Middle group, composed of the Yankton and Yanktonai tribes.

(3) The Lakota is the Teton or Western group, composed of the Oglala, Brule, Hunkpapa, Miniconjon, Sans Arcs, Sihasapa (or Blackfoot), and Two Kettle tribes.

The quote about the Indians turning down the offer to send their young men to school took place in 1744, when commissioners from Maryland and Virginia offered to send Indian boys to William and Mary College.

About the Editors

Kent Nerburn and Louise Mengelkoch are a husband-and-wife team experienced in both journalism and native American affairs.

Louise Mengelkoch is an instructor of mass communication at Bemidji State University, Bemidji, Minnesota; she has a master of arts degree in English. She worked as a reporter, columnist, and editor for several native American newspapers, and taught for three years at Pine Point, an experimental school for native American youth on the White Earth Ojibwe Reservation.

Kent Nerburn, a Ph.D. in theology and art, is director of Project Preserve, an award-winning education program in oral history on the Red Lake Ojibwe Reservation. He is a member of the National Indian Education Association and has served as consultant for curriculum development to the American Indian Institute in Norman, Oklahoma.

THE CLASSIC WISDOM COLLECTION
OF
NEW WORLD LIBRARY

AFRICAN AMERICAN WISDOM. Edited by Reginald McKnight.

AS YOU THINK by James Allen. Edited and with an introduction by Marc Allen.

THE ART OF TRUE HEALING by Israel Regardie.

LETTERS TO A YOUNG POET by Rainer Maria Rilke.

THE MIND OF GOD AND OTHER MUSINGS: THE WISDOM OF SCIENCE. Edited by Shirley A. Jones.

NATIVE AMERICAN WISDOM. Edited by Kent Nerburn and Louise Mengelkoch.

POLITICAL TALES & TRUTH OF MARK TWAIN. Edited by David Hodge and Stacey Freeman.

THE POWER OF A WOMAN. Edited by Janet Mills.

THE SOUL OF AN INDIAN AND OTHER WRITINGS FROM OHIYESA. Edited by Kent Nerburn.

THE CALL OF OUR BLOOD: THE WISDOM OF THE HISPANIC PEOPLE. Edited by Nicolás Kanellos.

THE WISDOM OF THE GREAT CHIEFS. Edited by Kent Nerburn.

THE WISDOM OF WOMEN. Edited by Carol Spenard LaRusso.

THE WONDERS OF SOLITUDE. Edited by Dale Salwak.

New World Library is dedicated to publishing books
and cassettes that inspire and challenge us to improve
the quality of our lives and our world. Our books and
cassettes are available at bookstores everywhere.
For a complete catalog, contact:

New World Library
14 Pamaron Way
Novato, California 94949

Phone: (415) 884-2100
Fax: (415) 884-2199

Or call toll free: (800) 972-6657
Catalog requests: Ext. 50
Ordering: Ext. 52

E-mail: escort@nwlib.com
www.newworldlibrary.com